# Rollicking on the River and Other Southern Ramblings

*by Mary A. Gervin*

RoseDog Books

PITTSBURGH, PENNSYLVANIA 15238

RoseDog Books
585 Alpha Drive
Suite 103
Pittsburgh, PA 15238
Visit our website at *www.rosedogbookstore.com*

ISBN: 979-8-88812-329-4
eISBN: 979-8-88812-829-9

# Rollicking on the River
and Other Southern Ramblings

# Table of Contents

## II. Finding New Roads

## III. Walk in a New Way

## IV.  Dreamers after Dark

# I. Making Connections

*Don't hesitate to go out on a limb sometimes; after all, that's where the fruit is.*

Evan Esar

# Realization

Realization
A remembrance of things past
Mind over matter

Realization
Changes at the last minute
Contingency course

Realization
A good man is hard to find
Anticipation

Realization
Journey to the edge of night
Unexpected twist

Realization
Best laid plans going awry
Disappointment dawns

Realization
Stranger in a foreign land
Alone and afraid

Realization
Garden of earthly delights
Affairs of the heart

Realization
The world is too much with us
Mounting confusion

# Nuisance or Nuance

A housefly buzzed by;
A noiseless, patient spider
Spun its silken web…

# Black Like Me

I am the black male
Well-acquainted with the night
Daunting the darkness…

I, a black woman
Witty, wise, and wonderful…
Daring in darkness

# Woman Perfected

Woman perfected
Warm…willing…wily…worthy…
Takes the breath away

# Examination

Examination
Truth is stranger than fiction
Crystallization

# Unbelievable

Curiosity
Wandering in distant fields
The magic is real

# Illumination

Illumination
Turning a mess into success
Certain slant of light

# Ingenuity

Ingenuity
Choosing a road less traveled
Serendipity

# Sheer Perfection

Appalachian Trail
Challenging Blood Mountain Peak
Scenic wonderland

Picture perfect views
Pristine natural setting
Spectacular sight

# Taking chances

Incessant dog barks
Alarm…greeting… or warning…
Something is amiss

# Wind song

Wind in the willows
The sound of nature breathing
Whispering softly

# Equilibrium

Concerted effort
Good plan coming together
Coordination

Reciprocity
Fellowship of faithful friends
Affability

Equilibrium
Taking the shape of water
Delicate balance

# Daunting Destiny

Daunting destiny
Following false premises
Inherit the wind

# Egomaniac

Egomaniac
Mad man who would be monarch
Leader of the lies

Egomaniac
Mad man who would be monarch

# Olympic Champion

Olympic athletes
A challenge to win the gold
With due diligence

# Adventure Time

Change of direction
Finding fresh roads to travel
A Search for solace

Stand among giants
Rising to meet the challenge
Soar like the eagle

# Delaying Tactics

Delaying tactics
Tomorrow's another day
Relish this moment

Procrastination
Whatever will be will be
All in due season

# Holstein Cows

Constant cud chewing
Ruminating big bovine
Making wholesome milk

# Archeology

Archeologist
Peeling back layers of time
Paydirt from the past

# Reasonable Doubt

Realization
Nothing new under the sun
Reasonable doubt

# Abomination

Abomination
Something wicked this way comes
Sense of urgency

Apocalyptic
Appalling atrocities
Astronomical

# Tongue Wagging

Loose lips spew half-truths
Whispered words behind closed doors
Gossip mongering

Notions in motion
Spread like a chain reaction
Now run and tell that…

# Giant Ant

I saw a cow ant
Red thorax and abdomen
Racing on stick legs

# Southern Charm

Hospitality
Soul food…warm smiles…rustic life…
Laid-back southern style

# Radium Springs Retreat

Shady, mossy oaks
Cool, crystal-clear spring water
Refreshing retreat

# Spiritual Man

Spiritual man
Ye are the salt of the earth
New creature in Christ

Rejoice in the Lord
Ye are the light of the world
Dispelling darkness

# American Breadbasket

Stretches of farm fields
Corn, soybeans, cotton, peanuts…
Pastures of plenty

Silos of grain crops
American breadbasket
Feeding the hungry

# Emancipation

The fog has lifted
Light at the end of tunnel
Emancipation

The fog has lifted
Light at the end of tunnel

# Philadelphia

Philadelphia
City of brotherly love
The wonder within

# Experience Amazing

Walk on the wild side
Experience amazing
Extraordinary

Visibility
Something wicked this way comes
Unpredictable

# Uninhibited

Uninhibited
Dance like nobody's watching
With abandoned glee

# Sea Dragon

Tiny sea dragon
Water-colored camouflage
Hiding among weeds

# Music to the Ears

Do I hear raindrops
Pattering on the rooftop
Plip, plop, plip, plopping

Music to the ears
The rhythm of the raindrops
Sleepy serenade

# Disillusionment

Disillusionment
The world is too much with us
Valley of shadows

# Starry Night

Clear starry night sky
Twinkling miniature light show
Nocturnal wonder

# Restoration

Restoration route
Long road to recovery
A glimmer of hope

# Creatures of Habit

Creatures of habit
Honeybees…ants…lady bugs…
Taking to the task

# Chameleon

Chameleon reptile
Hidden color camouflage
Long-bodied and lithe

Lone little lizard
Torn tail reticulation
Benign bug-eater

# Living Legacy

Live a great story
Leave your space a better place
Conscientiously

# Possibility

Possibility
Adventures in wonderland
Flirting with danger

# Change of Pace

Insinuation
Turning sour grapes into wine
Transformational

# Too Far Gone

Freedom of the press
Enemy of the people
Misinformation

Breaking news headlines
Artificial memories
Breach of confidence

# Catalyst for Change

Catalyst for change
Sparking a revolution
A change of the norm

# II. Finding New Roads

*Happiness is a way of travel, not a destination.*
*Roy Goodman*

# Just Wondering...

Hello! How are you this fine day?
I'm sending a few lines your way
Had a feeling you were needing
A ray of hope amid skies of gray.

Has sunshine taken a holiday?
Do you miss its warmth, its glow?
Dark clouds will pass, blue sky again
Smile! Simply let joy overflow.

Stuck inside, moping around?
Ignore the late-breaking news
Sing a child's song of sixpence
Press through those moody blues.

# Just a Note

Just thinking of you today
Thought I'd drop a line to say
Though times may become tough
Day and night seem equally rough
Mind is torn, feeling forlorn
Don't fret over small stuff
Resist the urge to moan and groan
For you, dear friend, are not alone…

Remember, simply do not forget
A rainbow after a thunderstorm
Is not something to regret
Consider the flip side and concede
A half-empty glass is half full indeed.

One thing under the sun is a sure bet
The spirit of the Living Word
Abides with us yet…
Abides with us yet…

# Hope Springs Eternal

Are you hurt or dispirited
Ev'ry day the same old grind?
Has a sad report you've gotten
Caused you to wince and whine?
Has the joy of living faded
As gloomy days linger long?
Do you carry a shroud of grief
Cause you feel you have been wronged?

Do not wallow in self pity
Do not sing such a sad, sad, song.
Stand strong; be of good courage
Hope dawns as the morning sun.

Here's wishing you:
A brighter day
A lighter heart
A warm smile
May they thwart
Those blahs away…

Good vibes sent your way
To keep your spirits high
Hoping to brighten your day
As the hours drag by.

# God Bless You Today

God's blessings reign on you
As you're recovering:
God bless you in the morning
With a bright, cheery day
God bless you with a restful afternoon
God bless you in the evening, I pray
As peace and comfort resume.
God strengthen you and make you
Feel much better soon.

May God bless and keep you
And may His grace abide you
In all you're going through.
My prayer as you are confined:
God's favor find you at this time.

# Up and Down

The present situation is but
A temporary condition
If time seems stuck in a rut
The minute hand shifts in seconds.
Change is inevitable
Seasons come and seasons go
Life cycles are implacable.
Sea tides ebb; then sea tides flow.
Good times over, the bad ones come
Joy is fleeting; sorrows don't last
Wars begin; battles are won
Day in, day out, opposites clash
Hope for the best; this too shall pass.
Stormy times? Despite the pain
The joy of sunshine will come again.

# Salutations

I had you on my mind
So I thought I'd drop a line
I don't follow you on Facebook
And I don't text or tweet.
I don't know your cell number
Today, letter-writing isn't neat.
Hoping this card, oh so simple
Won't make you groan or grumble,
Or hang your head in sore defeat.
Hoping you're feeling fine and dandy
Moving steady when on your feet
Having something to suit your fancy
And keeping safe while on the street.
Bye, bye now; check with you later
Be good now; no hanky pranky.

May the Lord bless and keep you
Amid all you may go through
Come sunshine or through rain
Even heartache, despite pain
Remain faithful and true
Until we meet again…

# Greetings

*Glorious start at break of day*
*Rising with the salutary sun*
*Eager to face the day*
*Early birds chirp in chorus*
*Tunes amid the treetops*
*Impassioned, idyllic morning melodies*
*New chance to make a change*
*Give thanks for the breath of life*
*See sunlight peeking through the blinds*

In all things give thanks
It's going to be a great day!

# Happy Times

Hearing the tingle of children's laughter
Amiable, amicable, awesome acquaintances
Pleasant place for relaxation and reflection
Planned get-away to favorite haunt
Impassioned music from a playlist
Nice cool drink under a shade tree
Engrossed in an engaging escapade
Solving a puzzling problem
Serotonin satisfaction

# O! Happy Day

This is such a glorious day!
Rejoice and be glad
That the Lord so made it.
Cast out the air of discontent
Blocks the will; stifles the wit.
Radiate joy, hope, peace
See the good mood spread.
Help make this holiday
The best we've ever had!

# If and When

(adapted)


If you will walk with patience
Along the footpaths of your life
If you would only realize
Each deed comes with a price…

If you believe you can help
Shape the world you see
If you can sense that you create
Your own reality…

If you can recognize yourself
In another's hopes and fears
If you can feel empathy
For another's pain or tears…

If you can build trust
With the choices that you make
Then your journey will be of worth
Whichever footpaths you take…

Whatever your choices
Whatever you do
May the journey ahead
Be an adventure for you.

# Twice Blessed

Great day in the morning!
Rising with a joyful heart
Aware of my surroundings
Thankful for the breath of life
Identifying familiar objects
Thoughts of plans ahead
Unable to wait for an alarm to sound
Delighted at daylight dawning
Emboldened by the power of God.

Giving thanks for God's grace and mercy
Realizing the wonder of wakefulness
Acknowledging the opportunity for a second chance
Thankful for feeling in my limbs
Itching to get started
Touched by the sounds of life around me
Up and about the day's business
Delving into an uncertain future
Embracing the magic in this new day.

# Daily Word

I pen these lines for you today
My wish is that at work or play
You remain strong, reverent, true
Wherever you are…whatever you do
Whatever you say…whatever the need
You can fulfill; you can succeed.
Though you may struggle, even fall
The Lord is with you through it all.

God bless you, friend, through your day
Guiding your footsteps along the way.
Trust that God is always there
With you in spirit, He truly cares.

# Good News

Born a carpenter's son
To be ruler of all nations
The Holy and Just One
Revered Captain of Salvation

Strung on a cross at Calvary
Wounded for our transgressions
Bruised for our iniquities
But a glorified resurrection
Offers hope for sweet surcease,
Secures our souls for eternity.

# Get Well Wishes

Caring thoughts
Like colorful blooms
Warm the heart
And lighten gloom…

Dark clouds have silver linings
As the elders often said
Each dawn poses the promise
Of a brighter day ahead…

Wishing you:
Beaming rays
Peaceful days
Cheerful ways
Restful stays…
(During your recovery phase.)

# Warmest Regards

Hello! I just want to say
Hope you're doing well today.
I had you on my mind,
Thought I'd take a little time
To jot down this little rhyme…

May you awaken with a smile
Then make the day worthwhile
Dispel any gloom and doom
For time passes much too soon.
Seek the joy in this new day
Then share it freely come what may.
Spend the day so when it's gone
You've done nothing wrong
If tomorrow never comes.

# Down Time

Coddling my pet cat
Against my body on the divan
Letting her take a well-deserved nap
Mealtime isn't going to happen.

Earlier she had tried
To help me read a book
When I ignored her antics
She gave me a sullen look.

She meowed for attention
When that didn't work
She pawed at my hand
As if her feelings were hurt.

# Just for Today

Disregard all the negatives
Accentuate the positives
Express love for the haters
Tune out the naysayers.

Scale down the noise
Of spiteful girls and boys
With charm and grace and poise
Exude the joy that love employs.

# Never Alone

You are not forgotten
Nor are you forsaken
Along life's journey
Snags may happen.

You are not forgotten
Nor are you forsaken
The Lord is great
And full of compassion.

You are not forgotten
Nor are you forsaken
Despite any darkness
Rays of hope beckon

Thinking of you
And wishing you well
Hope your day ahead
Will turn out swell.

# Heart to Heart

A bouquet of live flowers
All scented and pretty
Such expressions of regard
Soon fade in beauty

Gracious words of remembrance
Of kindnesses spoken
Or written on printed cards
Represent a token
To console, cheer or strengthen
Another's spirit that's broken
Or warm a heart that's frozen.

Here's hoping these words
Will do their part
Because they come
Straight from the heart.

# Speaks the Dawn

Hello morning! How are you today?
*Just fine, I'm proud to say.*
*I'm sending you folks blue skies*
*To start you on your way.*
*Not a rain cloud in the skies*
*To blot the scenic sunrise.*
*But if the sun proves too hot*
*With its piercing beta rays*
*Seek a shady resting spot*
*Just let the sunshine have its way.*

# An Evening Prayer

(adapted)

If I have uttered idle words, been vain
If I have judged another with disdain
If I have caused any distress or pain
Dear Lord, forgive.

If I have been perverse, or hard, or cold
If I did not seek peace within the fold
If I've defied your will, Almighty God
Dear Lord, forgive.

Forgive me for my debts, my trespasses
Bestow on me, O Lord, your blessedness
Lead me in the path of righteousness
Dear Lord—Amen.

# Nobody But the Lord

Wasn't it you, Lord, who made the sun to rise?
Wasn't it you, Lord, who colored the blue skies?
Wasn't it you, Lord who set the earth's tides?
It was you, Lord. Bless your name.

Was it you, Lord, who answered Ezra's cries?
Was it you, Lord who was Jacob's guide?
Was it you, Lord who opened blinded eyes?
It was you, Lord, bless your name.

It is you, Lord, who walks by my side
It is you, Lord, who knows what and why.
In you, Lord, I can always confide
Nobody but you, Lord, praise your Holy Name.

# Come Mourning

Lord, look down with tender mercy
While our dear one has passed away
Help us bear this grievous loss
Be our bulwark, boon, mainstay…

Lord, lift our hearts from this despair
Surround us with amazing grace
Fill us with thy Holy Presence
As we traverse this troubling space…

Lord, shine on us thy light of love
As we weep and mourn and sigh
Surrounded by thy loving-kindness
As we bid a last goodbye…

Lord, our dear one has departed
From this earthly realm of toll
Grant us hope that with tomorrow
The joy of being will unfold…

Lord, our dear one has departed
From earthly labor he is set free
Though we grieve at his transition
May we put our trust in thee…

Lord, our dear one has departed
From a world of sickness, of strife
Let the bereaved herewith remember
He has had an abundant life.

# Be Well

May God, the creator of all
All-knowing, Ancient of Days
Guide you through this pitfall
And strengthen you, I pray.

May God, our hope in ages past
Our strength for years to come
Buoy you for this bitter blast
And moor you amid the storm.

May God bless and keep you
Within the shelter of his arms
Through grace God will sustain you
And quell any arising alarm.

# Day by Day

A day without pain…
Is awesome wonder
A day without fear…
Is a time to hold onto
A day without regret…
Has moments without blunder
A day of compassion…
Makes friendships stronger
A day with laughter…
Makes life last longer
Moments of peace…
No time to squander
Moments of joy…
Bring memories to ponder
And make hope spring eternal

# Cheers

Chasing away those moody blues
Having a stiff drink of vodka
Enjoying tunes from my playlist
Eating a bunch of carb-laden treats
Resting on my chaise lounge
Smiling as I fritter the hours away.

# Christmas Greetings

Though it seems hard to believe
It's more blessed to give than to receive
Herewith, in this simple greeting
Don't be displeased
When yuletide is fleeting
A joyful heart—never aggrieved.

# At Christmas Time

Christmas is a time of giving
A time to embrace the joy of living
Christmas is a time for sharing
Gifts of love, a spirit of caring.

As you marvel at the wrappings
Look beyond the fancy trappings
Search inside and take due measure
A pure heart, the greatest treasure.

May God's grace abide within your home
When with loved ones or if alone
And may He sustain you long
After the holidays are gone.

# On Christmas Joy

Extending greetings to you and yours
Let peace and hope and joy
Spread throughout your home
And far beyond your own doors.

May the gift of love
By the blessed Savior's birth
Abide in your heart
And over all the earth.

# Christmas Blessings

Open your heart at Christmas
And not just your presents too
Let the spirit of the holidays
Propel your presence to produce
Goodness for those around you.

For generosity, love, and time
We pick and choose to share
When the yuletide has ended
Continue rendering tender loving care.

# Bless Your Heart

There are so few
Kind souls like you...
Ones willing to
Slog selflessly through
And minister to
Battered souls who
May be feeling blue
And wish they knew
A generous heart so true.

May God richly bless you
For all you do.

# My Wish for You

Wishing you well
Today and always
Praying God grant you
During the coming days
Whatever you need
To relieve this phase.

May you have:
Courage for the journey
Strength from above
May you feel God's presence
And be blessed by His love.

# With Appreciation

Although it seemed
I was ungrateful
My face beamed
When a few faithful
Honored me
Belatedly—
Making sure my birthday
Surely wasn't the worst day
And caused me to rant and scream
But one exceeding my wildest dreams!
Thanks so much for your thoughtfulness.
For your generosity may you be blessed.

# Neighborly

Nice neighbors next door
Elderly couple approaching their eighties
Insisting on living independently
Going about their daily duties
Household chores are equally shared
Busily keeping boredom at bay
On sunny days soaking up some sunshine
Really aging gracefully
Relying on God's goodness.

# With Heartfelt Condolence

In the coming days ahead,
After stacks of condolences are read,
All the congregants have been fed
And throngs of well-wishers have fled,
Cast your burden at the Master's feet
Trust Almighty God will meet
You at the Mercy Seat.

# III. Walk in a New Way

*The time is always right to do what is right.*
*M. L. King, Jr.*

# Rollicking on the River

Trembling waters seeking surcease
Tumbling currents flow lazily.
River rafting or paddle boating idly
Racing along the ripples on water skis
Intercepting the rapids in kayak slim
Boating or fishing for fresh perch or bream
Up and down the meandering banks or through the shoals
Herons and egrets for a meal troll.
As the river 's course is run,
Rollicking on the river in the sun
Hour after hour all day long.

# Flint River Ramblings

Flowing forward, gouging a southward trail through the earth
Rippling along its water route wild and free
Imposing its will with eddies, currents, undertow…
Neither man-made dam nor nature's wrath
Tamps its perpetual pulsing pursuit.
Rolling with dogged determination downstream
Illusive in its serene façade
Veiled threat from decaying tree stumps
  and vacillate depths in wet season
Elysian effect of bobbling ripples
Roll on rugged river, roll on.

# In Awesome Wonder

No wonder the poet said:
'I must go down to the sea again.'

Dawn eases into the morning sky
Azure dome hovers above restless gulf waters
Wave after wave wash sandy shore.
A slight breeze stirs the sultry air
Puffy clouds waft across the wide blue yonder
Seagulls sore across the blue expanse
The sun peeks slowly above the skyline,
Painting the sea shades of blue, green, teal
And the clouds tones of pink and pale gray.
A beachcomber strolls the silken sands.
An early-rising couple treads the water's edge.
Another couple erect a canopy to block the encroaching
        sun rays

Idle beach loungers, stacked in neat rows, align the
  water's edge.
Behind the stacked chaises, the sedge and bayou grasses peek
Through windswept dunes guarding against erosion.
What a magical mystical morning at Sunrise Beach.

# Summer Get-Away

At Sunrise Beach
Leaving worries behind
Blue skies and puffy clouds
In a relaxed state of mind…

At Sunrise Beach
Vacation has begun
Splashing in Gulf waves
And having tons of fun…

At Sunrise Beach
Combing the beach sand
Seashells in abundance
Colors washed bland…

At Sunrise Beach
Getting a golden tan
Sunshine unrelenting
More than I can stand…

At Sunrise Beach
Looking for cover
Temperature rising
Running to the water…

At Sunrise Beach
Baking in the heat
Skin turning brown
Like hearty roast beef…

At Sunrise Beach
Back at the hotel
Cool air conditioning
Sure does feel swell…

At Sunrise Beach
Perched on balcony
Looking at sunbathers
Basking in the heat.

# On Post

I work barefooted
In the sand
I work bare-chested
Sporting a tan.
I work early
I work late
On my job
I don't gain weight.
I see people
Come and go
Some are families
With kids in tow.
Bodies of all shapes and sizes
Different garb and hues
Various nationalities
Assorted demeanor, too.
I am a lifeguard
Holding the line
Jump right on in
The water's just fine.

# Gray Day

Voluminous cumulus clouds looming
Blanketing the sun,
Gray-tinged and smokey
Laden with moisture
Wafting…
Gathering…
    Rolling…
Impending rain…

# To an Octopus

Deep sea denizen
Eight-armed cephalopod
Intelligent marine mollusk
Lone eye gauging the watery depths
Tentacles laden with suction cups
Operating independently of brain
Navigating the coral reef habitat
Squirting an ink cloud
Darting away
Master escape artist

# Just Asking

Beachcomber, beachcomber
What did you find today:
A lost ring, beloved keepsake
Someone's treasure lost at play?
Should you return or report it?
Will you keep it for yourself?

Finders keepers; losers weepers
Enough said; nothing else left.

# Still Wondering

Why didn't the workmen set out the beach
       loungers this morning?
My, my!  What's going on?
Are the beaches closed today?
Is the surf too angry?
Currents too strong?
Along the shore red flags wave in the wind.
Still daredevils challenge the turbulence,
Flirting with danger.
Evidently, they're strong swimmers
Or people harboring a death wish.
Adrenalin junkies…

# Fish Hawk

On wide-spread wings,
A fish hawk glides over the waves
Searching for food in the wafting water below.
Peering with laser-like intensity,
Swooping down with talons of precision,
Effortlessly plucking a catch from the depths.
Master fisherman at the sea.

# To a Pelican

Webb-footed pelican,
Weird-looking avian,
Short, stumpy legs
Heft plumed abdomen.
Elongated, expandable, pouched bill
Equipped with air ducts
As into water, it extends
Senses alert to fish at will.

# Relentless Waves

The sea seems angry this morning.
Wave after white-capped wave crash
    against a vulnerable shore.
The Gulf breeze churns three-foot waves,
    Rippling one after another
Driftwood, seashells, dead coral, and polished rocks
    bear the onslaught
Even the seagulls seem restless
Flouncing above the turgid waters
    Ripping…
      Roiling…
        Rippling…
          Rocking…
        Rolling…
      Rising…
    Falling…
Bulging…
    Churning…
      Churring…
        Restless…
          Relentless…
Ill-at-ease in paradise.

# Sunrise...Sunset...

Slowly...gradually...finally...
The sun bursts forth in the morning
        into the cloudless eastern sky
Distant stars fade from view
        obscured by Sol's striking rays
Peeking above the horizon
        teasing the skyline that blocks
        its full blaze of glory
It peels away the cover of darkness
        setting ablaze the morning sky.
Blurry shapes become distinct images
        in the dappled dawn.
Warming rays chase away any morning chill,
Drying the dew-laden flora.
Dawn emerges from slumber.

Half a world away, the sun is sinking...
Slowly...gradually...finally...
The sun settles below the skyline.
The cover of darkness creeps over the landscape.
Green treetops become gray silhouettes against a darkening sky.
Dusk surrenders to the darkness
And settles down for the night
Slowly...gradually...finally...

Oceans away, another day is dawning...
Slowly...gradually...finally...

# Down South

Home here in the South
Where children and wild bunnies play
Where farm fields are found
And small towns abound
And a relentless sun holds summer in sway.

Home here in the South
Where possums and squirrels sashay
Where gnats whorl around
And tractors harrow the ground
And fire ants are working always.

Home here in the South
Where red clay and dirt roads seem okay
Where plantations still thrive
And hay bales are dried
And fruit groves seem like a mainstay.

Home here in the South
Where pine trees cover hills and plains
Where there're cotton fields galore
And there're melons by the score
And good folk process sugar cane.

Home here in the South
Where cows graze on the sweet grass
Where the farmers till their crops
From dawn 'til the sun drops
Until seasons of harvest have passed.

# A Bit of Whimsy

Love bugs are back:
In the front yard
Not being discrete
Out on the highway
Trying to stop traffic.

Swarming and mating
It's what they do
A seasonal milieu—
How to control them?
I wish I knew.

# Indubitably

As the moon circles the earth
And the earth circles the sun
The earth tides ebb and flow
Since creation was begun…

As clouds drift across the sky
And birds sing in the trees
Winds blow as they will
And leaves waft in the breeze…

Seasons come and seasons go
Offspring often depart from home.
As the seconds tick off the clock,
Time and tide roll on.

# The Great Escape

Sail away with me
Oasis in the South Seas
Vicariously

Paradise on earth
Palm trees…sea breeze…sand and surf…
Aloha Hawaii

# Falkland Penguins

Aquatic shore birds
Penguins of Falkland Islands
Whooping and wobbling

Swarming on the rocks
Black and white tuxedo birds
Flightless fins swimmers

Paired for a lifetime
Sharing duties parenting
Withstanding the cold

# On a Clear Day

At this moment, the wind is calm.
Look up in the sky.
It's a bird, a plane; it's a cloud formation
Cottony cirrus clouds drift aimlessly across an azure expanse,
weightless, airy, feathery, puffy…
Creeping from west to east
Forming ethereal shapes:

      steamboat…

      spacecraft…

      paw prints…

      smoke rings…

      whirligig…

Maybe ghastly wraiths of bearded men

      A giant lobster…

      A rabbit's head…

      A swan…

      Puffy marshmallows…

      Even an angel on horseback…

There but a moment,
Then drifting away
Forever gone…

# Mosquito Serenade

*M*ercilessly it meanders
*O*bstinate little onery pest
*S*inging a whiny, whirring tune.
*Q*uickly on fragile, agile wings it flits
*U*ntil its heat-seeking radar
*I*dentifies a warm-blooded victim
*T*o land upon and attack…
*O*dd little helicopter bug.

# Farm Work

Feeding the hungry
Across world food markets
Raising livestock and seasonal crops
Managing the fertile soil and fallow fields
Earning a living by rising early and working late
Reaping a harvest
Staving off starvation.

# Rooster Rousing

Rising at daybreak
Out in the barnyard
Obstinate feathered fellow
Sentry for the chicken yard
Telling the farm animals to rise and shine
Every morning like clockwork
Rousing the farm with a cock-a-doodle-doo.

# Bug Business

I sit in the glider on the front porch
Sipping a cup of herbal tea
I glimpse a busy bumble bee
Buzzing among bright blooms
From petal to petal, it flits
(*Tasting a liquor never brewed*)
Wings whistling a sonorous song
Passing up red peonies and pentas
Preferring to lap the lavender largesse instead
Morning after morning before the dew dries in the sun
Bumble bee busy about a bug's business.

# Ant Village

The ants have gone underground
Much too hot in the soaring sun?
Dropped food crumbs remain undisturbed
Foraging ants are submerged, tackling inside duties:
The family keeps growing
Workers keep scurrying
Incessantly burrowing
The queen needs attending
The habitat expanding
The nursery needs nestling
The lair needs refurbishing
On the go…
To and fro…
Moving…
Tunneling…
Digging…
Shoving…

Above the ground
A sandy mound
Oops! one misstep
Fire ants abound...
Bare foot stung
Round after round.

# Alley Cat

Alley cat…alley cat…

Where are you going?
Where have you been?
Around the block
And back again?

Alley cat…alley cat
What did you see?
Another stray tomcat
Roaming wide and free?

Alley cat…alley cat
Seeking likely prey
Eek! There's a wee mouse!
Ah! You let it slip away!

# Wasps

Working warily, winged warriors
Attentive, alert, aggrieved…
Pack of hornets protecting the nest
Stab by savage stingers
Sally by steady scalding horde.

# Say the Word

Caw...caw...caw...
Is the crow cry
As he perches
In treetop high.

Honk...honk...honk...
Was the goose reply
As he waddles
While passing by.

Tweet...tweet...tweet...
Whistled the songbird,
Sitting on a limb,
Wanting to be heard.

Who...who...who...
Called a night owl.
Cheep...cheep...cheep...
Spoke the pea fowl.

Gobble...gobble...gobble...
Carped Tom Turkey.
Quack...quack...quack...
Squawked lucky Ducky.

Blah...blah...blah...
Shared the surly sheep;
Nurturing the notion
They are benign beasts.

Oink…oink…oink…
Squealed hefty hog.
Grr…grr…grr…
Warned alert guard dog.

Hee haw…hee haw…
Declared delighted donkey
As he regaled
The cordial cacophony.

The sounds rang out
The words animals speak
Mere babble no doubt
(Translated by a quantum leap.)

# IV. Dreamers after Dark

*I will go anywhere as long as it is forward.*
David Livingston

# A Tribute to My Mother

*M* is for manners used to teach me social skills
*Y* is for the yarns spun at times when I've been ill
*M* is for memories shared to last a lifetime
*O* is for opportunities given, my fortune to find
*T* is for training to prepare daily meals
*H* is for helping hands to guide, chastise, or heal
*E* is for examples set to follow along the way
*R* is for readiness to serve wherever we may

Put them all together they spell *my mother*
As long as I shall live, I'll show I love her.

# Scribbling

Sitting with pen and tablet near
Contemplating subjects to shape into rhyme
Remembering topics already broached
Interested in new venues, different vistas
Being baffled by writer's block
Blank state of mind
Long stretch just doodling with pen
Excellent idea emerges
Something soothing gains surcease at last…

# Killing Time

Sleeping in past the alarm
Pushing back the bed covers
Lolling on the edge of the bed
Gaining equilibrium from rising
Ordering thoughts whirling through my brain
Slouching into the kitchen
Pouring a cup of day-old coffee
Sliding it into the microwave
Venturing into the bathroom
Taking a warm shower and shaving my legs
Stepping out and donning a towel
Grabbing a toothbrush to clean my teeth, then flossing
Rinsing with a minty mouthwash
Swiping my cropped locks with a hairbrush
I trek back to the kitchen for my coffee.
Wouldn't you know it?
I took so much time with the bidet,
I have to reheat my left-over coffee.

# Atlantic Voyage

Ancestors sailed across a vast watery expanse
Fraught with wretched hardships and daunting dangers
Crammed from end to end within the bowels of the slavers' ships
Iron chains binding black body to body, restricting motions
Riddled with fear of the unknown
Riding ocean currents and braving relentless waves
Identity ripped from Nubian captives
Craving surcease from sorrows
Aching to hear the familiar sounds of family home life
Africa's beleaguered bounty
Bound for the Americas.

# Woman's Work

I have much to do today:
Wash last night's dinner dishes, prepare, eat breakfast, strip the bed
linens, sort laundry, load washer, make the beds…
*(Phone rings..goes to voice mail…)*
pay bills, dust furniture, vacuum carpets, prepare and eat lunch,
mop kitchen and bathrooms, plan and prepare for evening meal…
*(Phone rings…answer the call.)*

Where was I?
Busy as ever.
What have I got going on today?
I've been so busy thinking of all I need to get done
I'm still in my P J's lying here in bed.
So much to do, I didn't know where to start.

# Hoarding

Having stashed stacks of decades old magazines
On top of outdated copies of newspapers and advertising circulars
Vintage clothes bulging from open furniture drawers…
Auntie's living quarters were trapped in time.
Relics from the past occupied every inch of her bedroom
Dear to her heart were memorabilia from by-gone days
Even the stale air waited to exhale
Removal or rearrangement of anything met with swift rebuke
Serious time for a hoarder intervention.

# Arthur's Lament

Are you aching in the wintry blast?
Relying on salves or ointment
To sooth Arthur's harsh grasp?
Hefty loads depleting cartilage
Upset joints' mobility?
Rusty hinges now displace flexibility…

# Aching for Release

Oh Arthur…
My Arthur…
Why so mean and cruel?
You assault my body
You cramp my style
You gnarl my joints
You warp my knuckles
You hobble my steps
You tangle my toes
You harangue my hips
You crunch my knees
You gnash my backbone
You gnaw at my elbows
You pierce through my body like a lightning bolt
You are a steady frienemy I can certainly live without.
My hinges are sorely cringing
I wish I could apply some W-D 40.

# Painful

Packing a punch, pounding, pulsing, penetrating…
Aching head, sore muscles, stiff joints,
Broken heart, gaping wound
In various intensities and sundry places
Needing release from the onslaught

# Mr. Webster and Me

Mr. Webster, please help me out
I need a word or two
As my thoughts wander about,
I wish to call on you.

You are such a learned man
Well-spoken, timely, and true
(Mr. Roget— not much in demand
And not as popular, too.)

You are a writer's steadfast friend
Relied on like a brother
Desk companion to the end
And constant like a lover.

A computer thesaurus may be around
For some scribblers and scribes
But if the computer is down
Look for a trusted book with pride.

Thus, when I'm at a loss for words
I readily seek your advice
(Though you don't list a few things I've heard,
Your choices will suffice.)

# What in the World?

The world is too much with us
A writer penned long ago
Had he lived longer, I trust,
He'd express concern, I know.

I miss the good ole days
When books were printed and used
Best-selling page-turners put readers in a daze
A daily newspaper—the source of news.

A new age is under way
A virtual universe has spawned
Cyberspace, metaverse, gigabits array…
As digital reality supplants the norm.

# Brave New World

Nobody is above the law a sage said
Sooner or later the piper must be paid.
By which premise?
Whose law: God, nature, man?
Innocent often convicted;
Guilty doing whatever he can.

The script has flipped.
Alternative facts sold
Law-abiding hurt,
Downtrodden treated like dirt
Gullible used, even abused
Egos bruised
Dissenters persecuted unnecessarily
Natural order subverted
Perverted unnaturally
Right going wrong
Wrong considered right
What's going on?
Reality real surreal…

# Gratitude

I'm truly thankful for…
Sound mind to discern fact from fiction
Mobility and dexterity of limbs
Empathy for my brother's plight
Fresh air to breathe unobstructed
Enough time to get my tasks done
Common sense enough not to tackle more than I can handle
Leisure time to enjoy my many blessings
Not suffering undue pain or misery
Ample food to nourish my body
Tools to take care of my needs
Sunshine to brighten the day
Rain for crops and nurturing the earth
Farmers growing crops, grain, produce, livestock…
Harvesters reaping crops for market
Friends to listen, hear, share, console…
Open ears to hear and respond
Mouth to offer a well-chosen word to console, uplift, or
strengthen one another
Grateful heart and willing hands
Presence of mind to live within my means
Mindset and capacity to expand my horizons
and learn something new
Transportation to get back and forth, to and fro
Mindset to gift, not to grift
Affable neighbors
Ability to control my temper, tongue, and base temptations
Ability to ideate distant places, Edenic vistas, and unusual people
Desire to make my environment a better place

Aches and pains to remind me I'm still alive and kicking…
I'm grateful to be still here after overcoming a bout
        with long-Covid 19
And realizing I am truly blessed and highly favored.

# Life Lessons

           Momma's rule was *don't…*
Sass your elders
Disrespect older folk
Be pigheaded
Be a tattletale
Be a showoff
Leave home without telling me where you're going or when you expect to be back
           And *don't…*
Talk in church
Chew with your mouth open
Bite off more than you can chew
Play with matches
Borrow from Peter to pay Paul
Pass the first lick
Say mean things about people
Wipe your nose on your sleeve
Sneeze without covering your nose
Shift blame when you're at fault
Act like an idiot
Keep adding fat to the fire
           And *don't you dare…*
Be a nuisance
Take all day to tackle a task
Whine all the time
Be a troublemaker
Run inside a building
Waste time, food, water, anything
Let people take advantage of you

Be a crybaby
Take your eyes away from where you're going
Begrudge others…

She always reminded me
Be careful of what you say and do
You don't want your actions, you see,
To come back to haunt you.

Rules I heard from Momma
Could fill a book or two
Many I passed on to my kids
Now I share them with you.

# A Change in Season

Before Covid 19 we used to…
Hug our friends and acquaintances in greeting
Kiss each other's cheeks
Greet each other with a handshake
Drop in for a cup of coffee
Have face-to-face conversations
Gather for a business meeting or church service
Visit the sick and shut-in
Not be concerned about surface sterilization
Be unconcerned about checking body temperature at gatherings
Apply moisturizing lotion on our skin
Attend an acquaintance's funeral
Sing together in a choir
Purchase pregnancy tests

After Covid 19 we…
Fist bump or elbow tap in greeting
Wear face masks to hide features at gatherings
Nod our head or wave in greeting
Contact one another via social media, e-mail, or text message
Hold meetings through zoom calls
Send cards of remembrance or greeting
Disinfect surfaces in our homes, schools, businesses…
Check body temperature before congregating inside
Use hand sanitizer for protection
Send flowers of acknowledgement
Have a soloist render a song for services
Purchase covid test kits…

Seasons come; seasons go
As the tides ebb and flow
Change is inevitable
The past is irrevocable.
A mistake is forgivable.

# Way of the Road

<table>
<tr><td>Among school children…</td><td>Ride along…</td></tr>
<tr><td>Caution</td><td>Speed limit</td></tr>
<tr><td>Slow: children at play</td><td>No passing zone</td></tr>
<tr><td>Pedestrian crossing</td><td>Slower traffic keep right</td></tr>
<tr><td>School zone</td><td>Men working</td></tr>
<tr><td>Stop all way</td><td>Lane closed</td></tr>
<tr><td>No thru traffic</td><td>Move over</td></tr>
<tr><td>No U turn</td><td>Bridge ices before road</td></tr>
<tr><td>Bike lane ahead</td><td>Express lane ahead</td></tr>
<tr><td>Yield to right of way</td><td>Merging traffic</td></tr>
<tr><td>Right turn only</td><td>Acceleration lane</td></tr>
<tr><td>Keep off the grass</td><td>Caution</td></tr>
<tr><td>Limited access</td><td>Water on road</td></tr>
<tr><td>Dead end</td><td>Share the road</td></tr>
</table>

# American Discharge

Throwing out accumulated newspapers and uneaten leftovers
Rinds of watermelons, overripe fruits, rancid meat, rotten
      vegetables…
Any empty jars, bottles, cans, unwanted plastics…
Shredded mail, personal documents, cardboard boxes…
Tons of unwanted and discarded materials from neighborhoods
Headed for the garbage heap week after week
Population explosion
Discharge America
Waste management

# Motivation

Mentally making note of many lame excuses
Only to postpone the inevitable
Time to get the ball rolling
Ignore the imp inside the head
Voice of procrastination
Aiming to forestall forward progress
Taking charge of will power
Impetus to act instead of dawdling
Opportunity awaits
Nothing ventured; nothing gained.

# Lost World

Condition for concern
Occasional brain fog and memory lapses
Nothing familiar any longer
Failure to remember regular routines
Unclear perception of left and right
Sinister prognosis of a living hell
Into a time-warp
Oblivious to reality
Sentence of senility
Nightmare for the living

# Ready Or Not

Fretting about unforeseen dangers
Eschewing enjoyable events
Anticipating the worst outcome
Rising adrenaline
Ready or not
Fight or flee…

# Graduation Day

There is a time a season, a purpose
For all things under the sun
Today we've gathered to recognize
What a select few have done.

At this time, we look back on
What has brought you to this day
Problems faced; decisions made
And lessons learned along the way.

The goals set; the challenges met
Milestones reached; obstacles breached
The friendships made; great things done
Times of fulfillment; struggles overcome.

Today, we seek new opportunities
Another adventure to pursue
Assessing your present situation
From another point of view.

Henceforth may you find satisfaction
As you start on your career
A sense of true fulfillment
That grows greater with each year.

May the commitment that you've shown
And the knowledge you possess
Help you meet each opportunity
For achievement and success.

Graduates, in recognition of your victory
In celebration of your journey
In expectation for your future
We commend you for your achievements
And wish you Godspeed as you go forth
To fulfill your destiny.

# At Graduation

There is a time, a place, a purpose
For all events under the sun
Today we gather in this place
To celebrate the good work you've done.

Graduation day is an exciting time
A day of laughter, smiles, cheers…
Moments of fond farewell, even tears
Time for speeches, songs, applause
Handshakes, hugs; even taking pause
To share memories of the past
Making promises to remain steadfast
With close friends and family
Before assuming adult responsibilities…

Graduation is a day to be proud
Of all that you have learned
It's also a day to thank the good Lord
For that parchment you have earned.

Indeed, graduation day is many things
All wrapped up into one
A wish fulfilled; a milestone met,
A start to new adventures under the sun.

# What Is Graduation?

What is graduation?
A milestone, a crossroads, a goal achieved
A star to reach for
A diploma received

The ending of one dream
A new one begun
Recognition for all
The industry you've shown.

A happy event
An exciting fresh start
A time to feel proud
And follow your heart.

Now, we extend warmest wishes
That could ever be sent
And our sincere congratulations
On your fine accomplishments.

And here's hoping that your future
In ways both large and small
Will bring the things you've dream of
And wanted most of all.

# A Graduation Tribute

Greetings and salutations
Ring out bells of acclamation
Amid the entire congregation
Upon this select group before you.
Admire their drive, their will to push through.
Take them as an inspiration to pursue
Ingenious plans and infinite possibilities.
Offer them accolades if you please
Never doubt their exceptional abilities.

Days on end, graduates, you stayed the course
Achieved a sealed parchment, a diploma, of course.
You deserve far more than a round of applause.

# Elegy for My Brother

### (adapted)

How do you know the measure of a man?
Is it through the life he leads?
Is it through his path of integrity
That he never would deceive?

Do you know the measure of a man
When he looks into your eyes,
When his love and kindness fill you
And his spirit he can't disguise.

Can you see the measure of a man
Who smiles despite his pain
Who always embraces the sunshine
And laughs through all the rain?

I have seen the measure of a man
Whose family hold him dear,
Whose strength was inspirational
And regard always sincere.

I have known the measure of a man,
One who touched our heart,
Whom the angels softly spoke to
And who from us did part.

Remember that the measure
Of this man forsaketh not,
And the love he brought into our lives
Will never be forgot.

Softly we will speak of him
To chase the pain away,
And the love we share among us
Will unite us all some day.

# Epic Fail

Feat of the foolish
Preposterous plan to *stop the steal*
Incited by white noise from bigots
Assembly of discontented anarchists
Failure to quell the maddening crowd
Invasion of the Capitol Building
Wanton destruction and defacement of revered citadel
Last stand of left-wing radicals
Ending in disaster
Epic fail…

# Me, Myself, & I

Movement is my mantra
Yielding aches and woes, aha
Still, I'm up and moving around
Eager to keep the muscles sound.
Life is too short to waste time
Frittering the day away on my behind…
Even when I'm sitting, I find
I'm exercising my mind
Before it retreats far beyond
A surreal realm and into oblivion.

# Backward Glance

As a child I remember…

Being smaller than other children my age and having to be scrappy
and smart to outwit bullies who thought I was a weakling
Momma waking me early in the morning to get ready for school and
sharing a cup of coffee as I dreamed of riding the merry-go-round
during school recess
Our dog Bullet adopting our home after his owners abandoned him
near our house
Ole Bullet sneaking into the house and crawling under the bed to
escape thunderstorms raging outside
Rambling through the woods with my sister and picking
blackberries, huckleberries, persimmons, plums, eating 'til we were
full, then taking the rest home to Mama to make pies or to preserve
Waking on Christmas morning to see what Santa Claus had left
around the tree, then helping prepare the vegetables for cooking the
Christmas feast
Finally discovering that Santa Claus was Momma and Daddy when
I awoke early one Christmas to discover them putting out the pres-
ents for my sister and me
Moving to the outskirts of Columbus when my family was chased
from our country home by our deranged mule.

I remember…
going to a forbidden neighbor's house instead of staying at my
grandmother's and Momma and my sisters combing the neighbor-
hood for me, thinking I was lost, then my returning home hungry
and tired and being welcomed with open arms instead of getting a
spanking for my disobedience.

I recall…

playing hopscotch, pick-up sticks, jackstones to while away idleness, sometimes talking to my imaginary companion to quell loneliness when my sister started grade school without me.

smelling the pastries and feasting on fluffy peach puffs and fruit pies Momma baked in the wood stove for special occasions.

And I remember longing to be older and to get bigger so I could outgrow being called by my nickname:

*Tiny.*

# The Lighthouse

Lodged upon a rocky outcrop
Isolated close to shore
Giving warning of the shoals
Hazards the jagged shoreline posed
Twinkling stream of welcome light
Heading off disaster
Offering a safe harbor for incoming cargo ships
Up and down the shipping lane
Sturdy during strong winds
Early warning system

# Parris Island Proud

Protecting the imperiled populace
And guarding the Atlantic coastline
Radar scanning the distant vistas
Ready to jump into action
In case of threat by enemy forces
Safety ensured at sea

Preparing during peace time
Rigorous training of raw recruits
Odd assortment of fresh young faces
Until turned into a fighting machine
Daring and undaunted marines

# St. Simon Journey

Barrier island
The past is always present
Spanish settlement

Historical past
St. Simon Island journey
British incursion

Clash of two cultures
The Battle of Bloody Marsh
Tall tale told as truth

# Author Profile

***Mary A. Gervin*** is a retired English professor and writing consultant. Since her retirement, she has released three books of poetic works: *Trapsing into Twilight* and *Walking in Delight* through Doublexposure Media and *The Spinning of Moss* with Page Publishing. A native of Columbus, Georgia, the author settled in Albany along the Flint River after graduating from college in Atlanta. Later pursuing graduate study at Florida State University in Tallahassee, Gervin has worked as an English professor honing the skills of budding writers and poetry enthusiasts; served as a consultant for various textbook companies, writing councils and educational boards; and acted as adjudicator for national and regional literary competitions. *Rollicking on the River* is a volume of assorted poetic forms and themes and purposes with a Southern flavor. It contains verse for different occasions from birthdays and holidays to anniversaries and condolence. This volume also expresses sentiments about nature and the world around us. *Rollicking on the River*, in addition to copies of Gervin's other books, is available wherever books are sold.

www.ingramcontent.com/pod-product-compliance
Lightning Source LLC
Chambersburg PA
CBHW060929140726
47996CB00001B/435